Weather Watch!

THE WEATHER
IN
SPRING

Miriam Moss

Wayland

Weather Watch!

Other titles in this series include:
The Weather in Summer
The Weather in Autumn
The Weather in Winter

Cover pictures: (Main picture) Wild spring daffodil. (top left) Male chaffinch with his hungry babies. (centre) Pear tree in Saargau, Germany. (bottom right) Spring lamb.

Contents page: A beautiful and colourful spring rainbow arcs across a field of ripening corn. But in the distance, stormclouds gather.

Editor: Deb Elliott
Designer: Malcolm Walker

Text is based on *Spring Weather* in the *Seasonal Weather* series published in 1990.

First published in 1994 by
Wayland (Publishers) Ltd
61 Western Road, Hove
Sussex, BN3 1 JD, England

© Copyright Wayland (Publishers) Ltd

British Library Cataloguing in Publication Data
Moss, Miriam
  Weather in Spring. - (Weather Watch! Series)
  I. Title II. Series
  551.6

ISBN 0-7502-1182-2
Typeset by Kudos
Printed and bound by Casterman S.A., Belgium

CONTENTS

FOUR SEASONS 4
WARMING THE EARTH 6
HERE COMES SPRING! 8
THE AIR ABOVE US 10
IT'S WINDY! 12
IT'S RAINING! 14
COLD AIR MEETS WARM AIR 16
THE SEASON OF SPRING 18
SPRING SURPRISES! 20
SPRING RAINBOWS 22
THE HOLE IN THE SKY 24
WEATHER MAPS 26
HOW TO MEASURE RAINFALL 28
GLOSSARY 30
BOOKS TO READ 31
INDEX 32

FOUR SEASONS

Look at the map below. Can you see that it is always cold at the North and South Poles? The weather is usually warm in the tropical countries which lie in the middle band of the world.

In between the Poles and the tropics are temperate countries. These countries have four clear changes in the weather during the year, called seasons. The four seasons are spring, summer, autumn and winter.

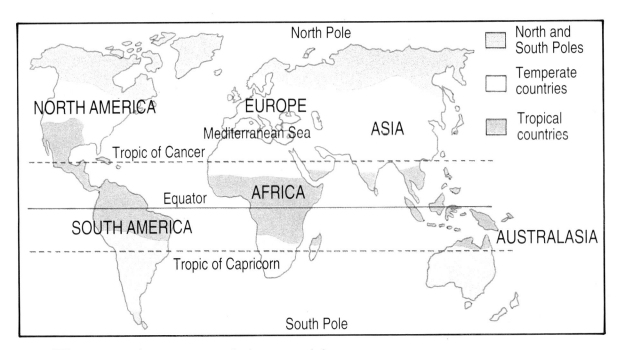

↑ *The weather around the world.*

⬆ *Bright flowers are one of the first signs of spring.*

Spring is the first season of the year. It comes after the short, dark days of winter. In spring the air feels warmer and the Sun sets later each evening.

HERE SOMES SPRING!

Spring comes as the Earth turns towards the warmth of the Sun. The spring sunshine melts the winter snow and ice. Sometimes rivers cannot hold the newly melted water which bursts over the riverbanks. This is called spring flooding.

In the mountains in spring huge amounts of snow melt in the sunshine. The snow becomes loose and crashes down into the valleys below. These dangerous snowfalls are called avalanches.

← *Farmers plough their fields ready for planting crops in spring.*

← *In spring low cloud and mist hang over the mountain tops.*

An avalanche crashing down a mountain slope. ➡

Guess how fast the snow in an avalanche travels?

The snow in an avalanche in Switzerland travelled at 349 kilometres an hour.

THE AIR ABOVE US

The air around the Earth is called the atmosphere. It is made up of many different gases. The gas we need to breathe is oxygen.

The air in the atmosphere presses down on the Earth's surface. This is called air pressure. Different air pressures bring different kinds of weather.

Ozone is an important gas found high up in the atmosphere. It protects us from the hamful rays of the Sun.

Temperatures through the atmosphere. ➡

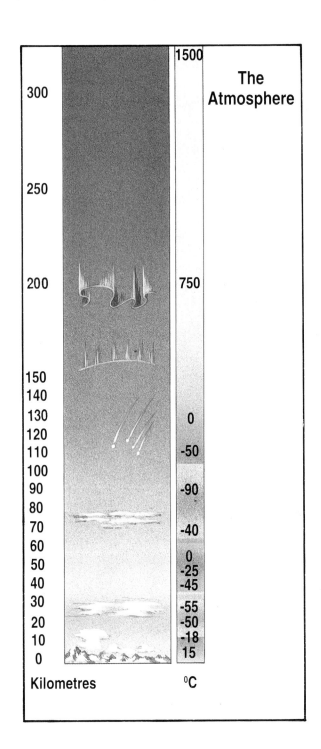

The Atmosphere

Kilometres		°C
300	1500	
250		
200		750
150		
140		
130		0
120		
110		-50
100		
90		-90
80		
70		-40
60		
50		0
40		-25
30		-45
20		-55
10		-50
0		-18
		15

↑ *From space you can see the clouds swirling above the Earth.*

← *Hot air rises. This balloon is filled with hot air so it floats up into the sky.*

IT'S WINDY!

Wind is air that moves about, but what makes the air move?

Some places on Earth have warm air above them, others have cool air. Cool air is heavier than warm air, so cool air sinks. The warm air rushes into the spaces left. This rushing air is the wind blowing.

⬇ *Different winds around the world have their own special names. Look at the map below to see the different winds and where they blow.*

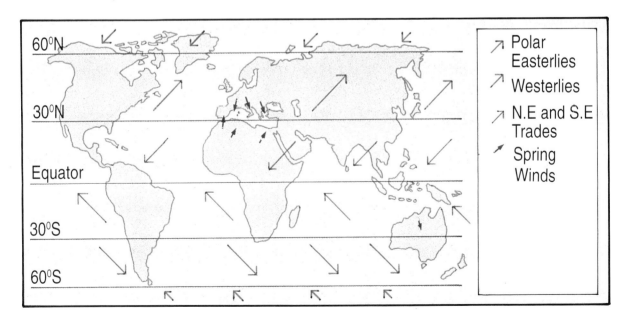

There is a famous cold, north wind, called the mistral, which blows down the River Rhône in France in spring each year. ➡

⬅ *Can you see from the shape of this tree which way the wind usually blows?*

IT'S RAINING!

When the Sun warms the sea, some of the water turns into water vapour. (You can see water vapour as steam when a kettle boils.)

The water vapour rises up and cools, turning into tiny droplets of water. Clouds are made of these tiny droplets. When the water droplets grow too heavy, they fall to the ground as rain. Hail and snow are really frozen rain-drops.

← *It may be spring, but these dark clouds are bringing a rainstorm.*

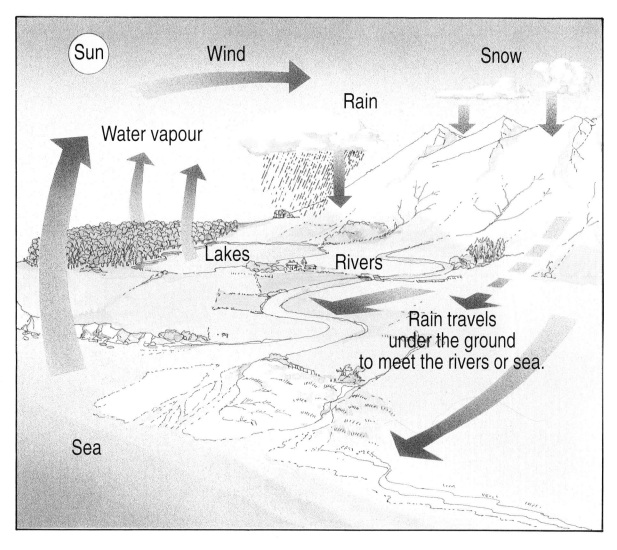

Labels within diagram: Sun, Wind, Snow, Rain, Water vapour, Lakes, Rivers, Rain travels under the ground to meet the rivers or sea., Sea

⬆ *Water from seas and lakes becomes clouds, falls as rain or snow, sinks into the earth and is carried by rivers back out to sea.*

Clouds are always changing shape as they move through warm or cold air. They shrink or grow as the water vapour, which you can't see, turns to droplets, which you can see - and back again.

The air around the Earth is always moving. It rises when it is warmed by the Sun and it sinks when it is cooled down. Warm air and cool air do not mix. When they meet it is called a front.

Can you see from the diagram below that different kinds of clouds form on warm fronts and cold fronts?

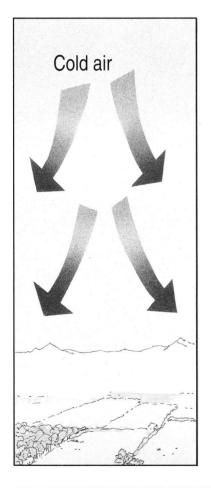

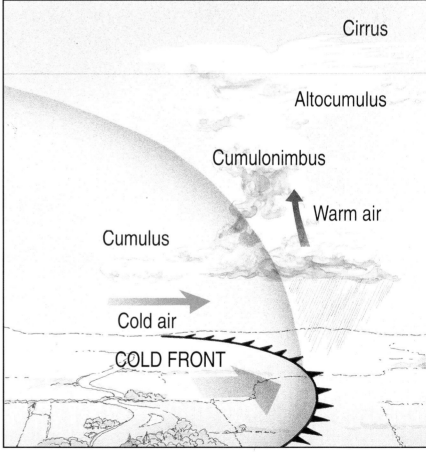

Cold fronts move slowly because cool air is heavier and more difficult for the wind to move. During spring weather, bright sunshine follows rain showers because warm fronts and cold fronts follow on one after the other.

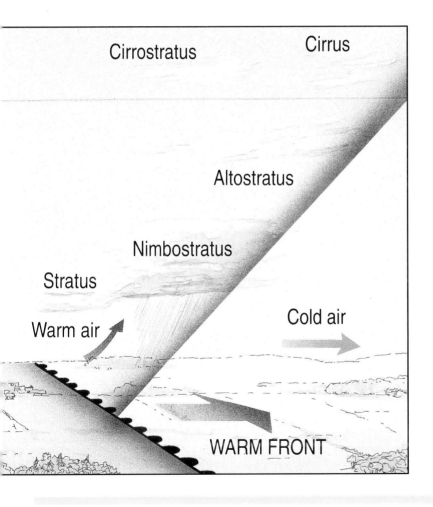

← The heavier, cold air of the cold front pushes the warm air upwards. Clouds form and then it rains.

THE SEASON OF SPRING

Spring in temperate countries usually lasts for about three months. In northern Europe it lasts from April to June.

↓ *Huge fields of tulips grow in the Netherlands in spring.*

↑ *Spring in an Italian harbour on the Mediterranean Sea.*

In countries around the Mediterranean Sea the unsettled spring weather lasts from March to May.

Spring comes late in the year at the North and South Poles. The snow may not start to melt until late in May. There can be snowstorms at the North Pole as late as the middle of June.

↓ *In winter this sea is frozen solid. In spring the ice melts leaving these unusual shapes.*

SPRING SURPRISES

Spring is full of surprises. It brings sudden changes in the weather to many parts of the world.

↓ *When the spring rains fall on African deserts, like the Kalahari Desert below, a carpet of flowers appears in the sand overnight.*

Strong warm winds sweep across the Great Plains of northern USA in spring. They bring fierce tornadoes which uproot trees, overturn cars and hurl houses into the air.

Planting rice in Thailand before the heavy monsoon rains arrive. ➡

⬇ *The long tail of this spring tornado whirls through the evening sky in the USA.*

Over 500 people were killed, 6000 more were hurt, and hundreds of thousands lost their homes when a spring tornado hit Bangladesh in 1977.

Sunlight is made up of seven colours - red, orange, yellow, green, blue, indigo and violet. If the Sun shines when it is raining, the raindrops break up the sunlight into these seven colours. We see this as a rainbow.

↓ *To find a rainbow, stand with the Sun behind you and look towards the falling raindrops.*

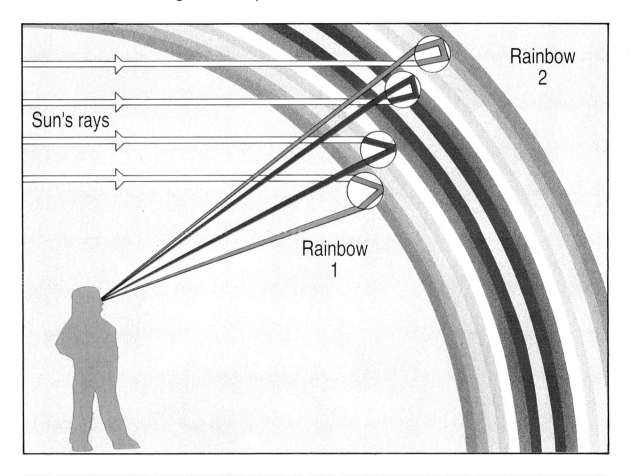

← Sun + rain = rainbows!

When the Moon shines through thin clouds, the water droplets in the clouds split the light into coloured bands. This shows up as a coloured ring around the Moon. ➡

THE HOLE IN THE SKY

We are protected from dangerous ultraviolet rays from the Sun by a thin layer of gas in the atmosphere. This important gas is called ozone.

We use chemicals called CFCs in spray cans, fast-food wrappings and fridges. CFCs collect over the South Pole during the still, dark winter. As soon as spring arrives, the Sun in the Antarctic helps the CFCs to attack the ozone layer and make holes in it.

↓ *This picture of Earth shows a hole in the ozone layer over the South Pole. The hole is the white area with black in the middle.*

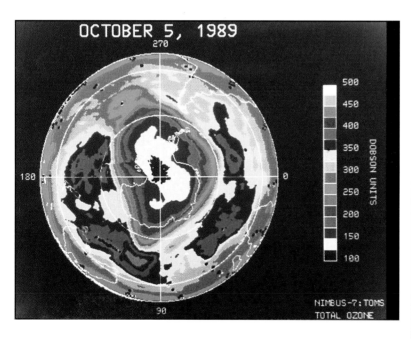

In 1989 the hole in the ozone layer over the South Pole was the same size as the USA.

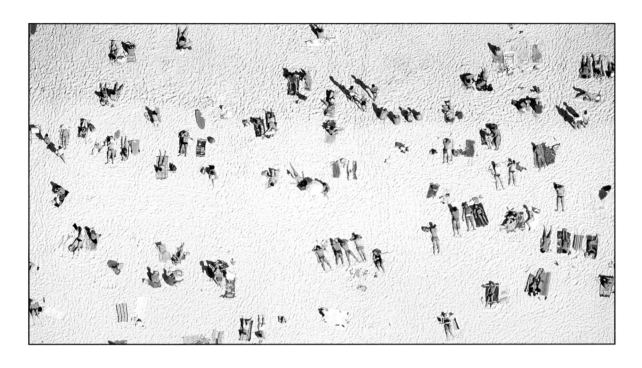

↑   *These sunbathers in Australia are soaking up dangerous ultraviolet rays from the Sun.*

We must stop using CFCs and protect the ozone layer.

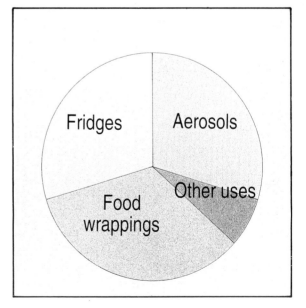

CFC chemicals are used all over the world.   ↑

25

We have all seen weather forecasts on television or read them in newspapers.

All over the world scientists collect information from ships at sea and from weather balloons sent high into the atmosphere.

Space satellites send pictures to weather stations. All this information is fed into computers and made into weather maps.

↑ *Fine spring weather in Texas in the USA.*

⬇ *High and low pressure bring different kinds of weather. This spring weather map shows high pressure over Texas in the USA.*

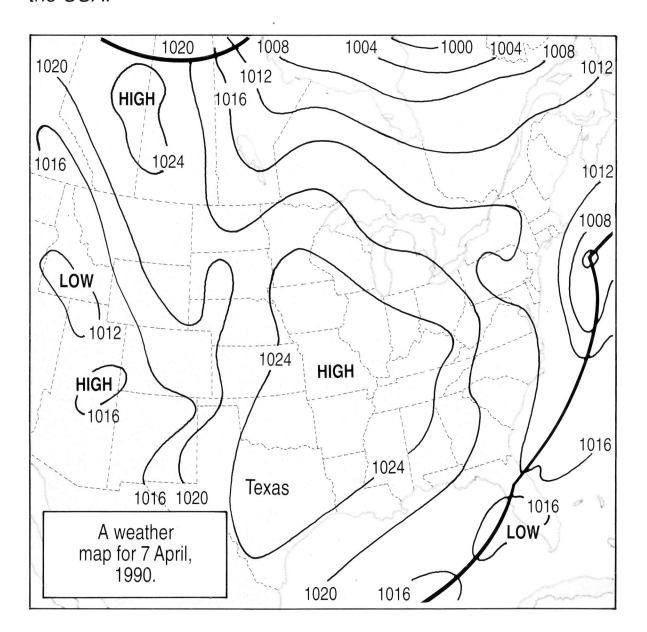

A weather map for 7 April, 1990.

You will need:
* a straight glass jar, 125 mm across the bottom.
* a plastic funnel, 125 mm across the top.
* a strip of white paper the same height as the jar, marked off in millimetres.
* waterproof sticky tape.
* some modelling clay.

1. Put the plastic funnel into the neck of the glass jar.

2. Press the clay into the neck to make the jar waterproof.

3. Stick the paper scale to the outside of the jar using waterproof tape. (Check that the bottom of the scale is at the bottom of the jar.)

4. Put the rain gauge out in the open, away from trees and buildings.

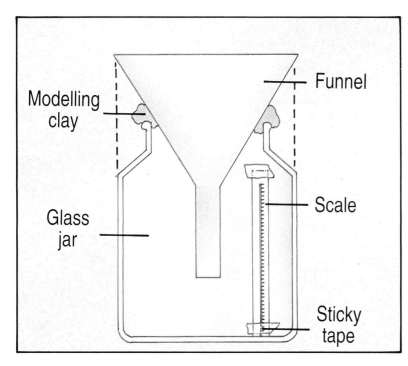

Modelling clay

Funnel

Glass jar

Scale

Sticky tape

← *This is what your rain gauge should look like.*

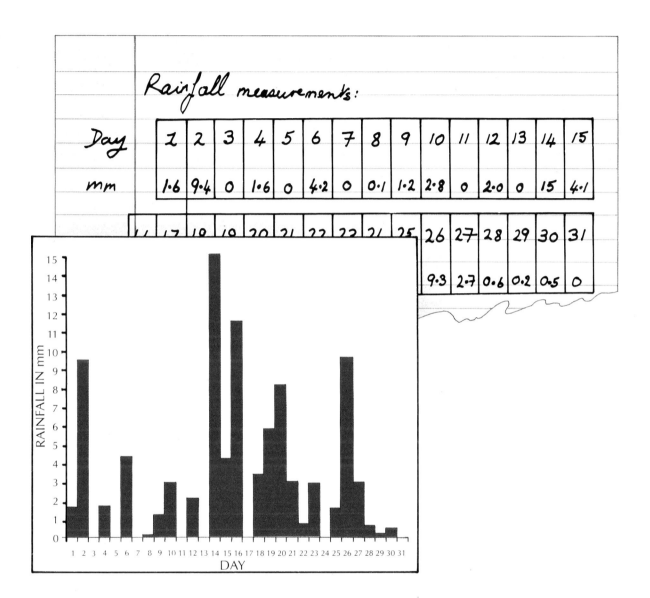

Rainfall measurements:

Day	1	2	3	4	5	6	7	8	9	10	11	12	13	14	15
mm	1.6	9.4	0	1.6	0	4.2	0	0.1	1.2	2.8	0	2.0	0	15	4.1

Day	16	17	18	19	20	21	22	23	24	25	26	27	28	29	30	31
mm											9.3	2.7	0.6	0.2	0.5	0

You can record the amount of rain you collect in the jar each day using a notebook or a bar chart.

GLOSSARY

CFCs Chemicals which can damage the gas ozone in our atmosphere. CFCs is short for chlorofluorocarbons.

desert Large areas of very dry land.

flood A large amount of water covering land. Floods are often caused by heavy rain.

forecast Something which lets people know about something before it happens.

funnel A hollow container with a wide mouth going down into a small tube. It is used for pouring liquids without spilling them.

meteor A small amount of rock-like material which enters the Earth's atmosphere. Meteors can sometimes be seen in the sky at night burning up before they hit the ground.

monsoon A wind that changes direction with the seasons. It often brings heavy rainstorms.

ozone A gas found high up in our atmosphere which protects us from some of the Sun's rays.

plough To prepare earth for sowing seeds by turning it over using sharp blades.

radiator A room heater made out of several metal tubes carrying hot water.

ultraviolet rays Invisible rays of sunlight which can damage our skin.

Books to read

Let's Celebrate Spring by Rhoda Nottridge (Wayland, 1994)
Projects for Spring by Celia McInnes (Wayland, 1988)
Rainy Weather by Jillian Powell (Wayland, 1992)
Spring Festivals by Mike Rosen (Wayland, 1990)
Weather and it's Work by David Lambert and Ralph Hardy (Orbis, 1988)
Windy Weather by Jillian Powell (Wayland, 1992)

Picture acknowledgements
Bruce Coleman Ltd cover, main picture (Dr Eckart Pott), centre (Hans-Peter Merten), bottom right (Hans Reinhard), 5 (Hans Reinhard), 19 (Bob and Clara Calhoun), 21 (top, C.B. Frith), 26 (John Shaw); J. Allen Cash 9 (top), 13 (both), 14; Frank Lane Picture Agency cover, top left (John Hawkins); Oxford Scientific Films 20, 23 (bottom); Photri 11 (top); Science Photo Library 24; Tony Stone Worldwide cover background, contents page 7, 8, 9 (bottom), 18 (both), 23 (top), 25; Topham Picture Library 21 (bottom); Zefa 11 (bottom). All artwork is by Malcolm Walker except page 6 which is by the Hayward Art Group.

INDEX

air pressure 10, 27
atmosphere 10, 11, 24, 26
Australia 7, 25
autumn 4, 7
avalanches 8, 9

CFCs (chemicals) 24, 25
clouds 14, 15, 16, 17

Earth, the 6, 7, 8, 10, 11, 12, 16, 24
Europe 7, 18

floods 8
flowers 5 20
front 16

Moon, the 23

North Pole 4, 19

ozone layer, the 11, 24-5

rain 14-15
  measuring 28-9
  monsoons 21
rainbows 22-3

seasons 4
South Pole 4, 19, 24
summer 4
Sun, the 5, 6, 7, 8, 11, 14, 16, 22, 23, 24, 25

temperate countries 4, 18
tornadoes 21
tropical countries 4

USA 21, 24, 26

weather
  forecasts 26
  maps 26-7
wind 12-13, 17, 21
winter 4, 5, 18, 19